# Kat and



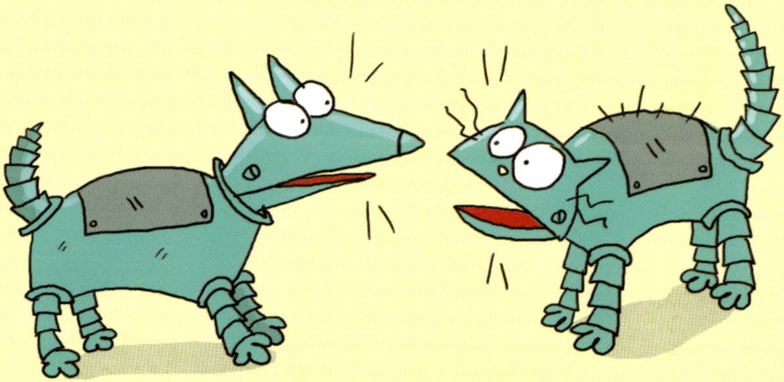

Written by Monica Hughes
Illustrated by Joëlle Dreidemy

RIGBY

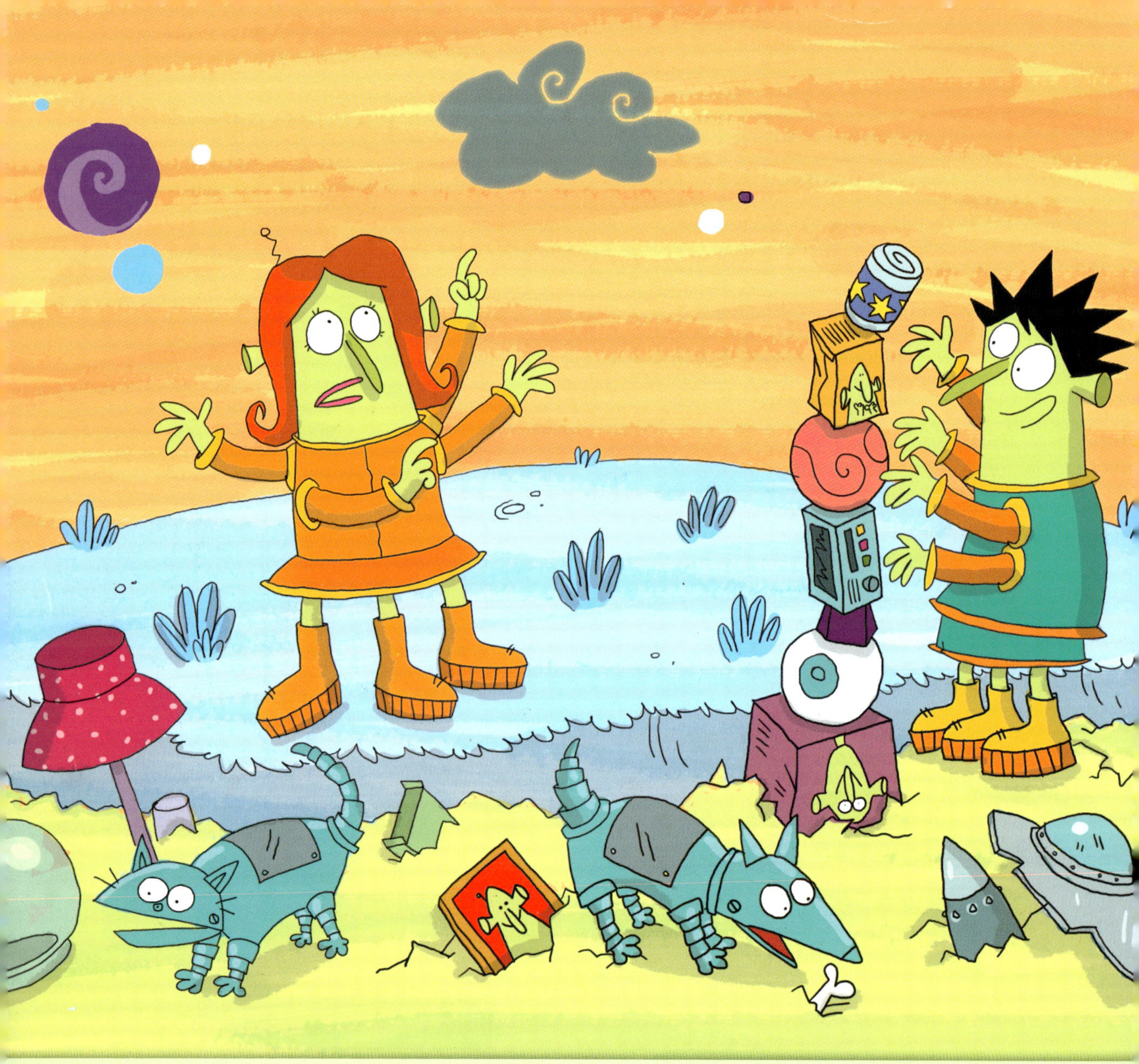

Kat and Dan nip to a tip.

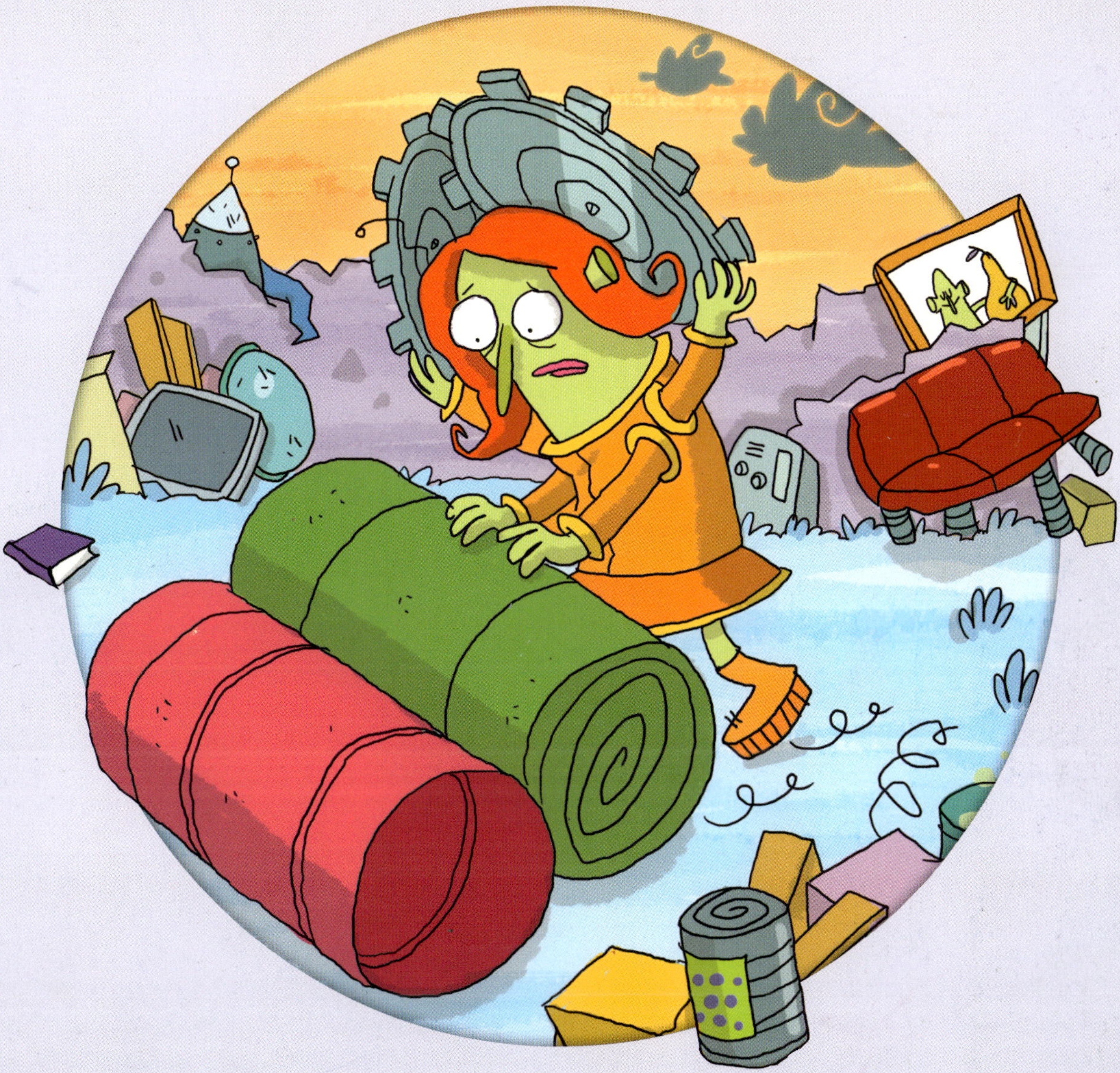

Kat got cans and cogs.

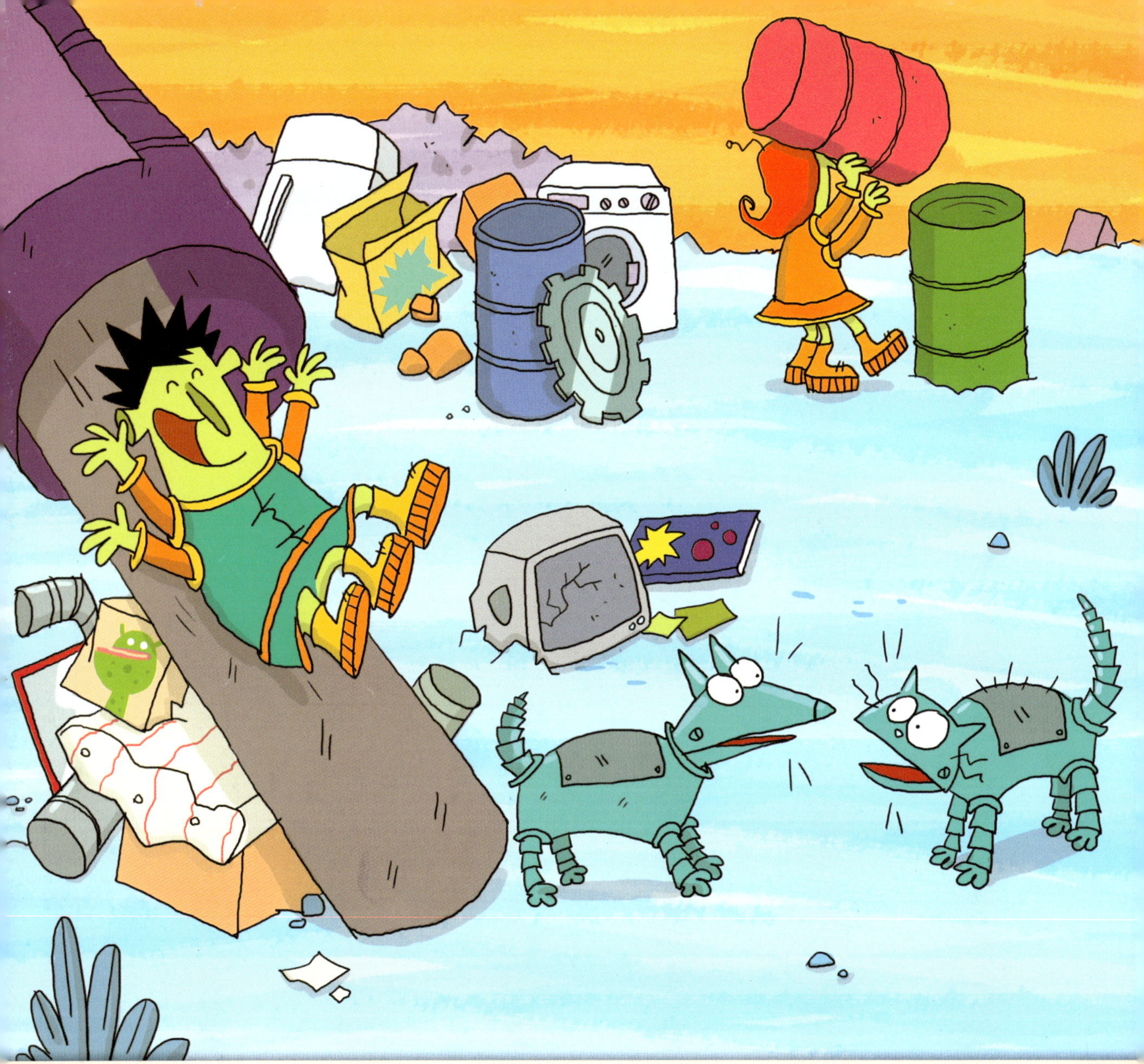

Dan did not.

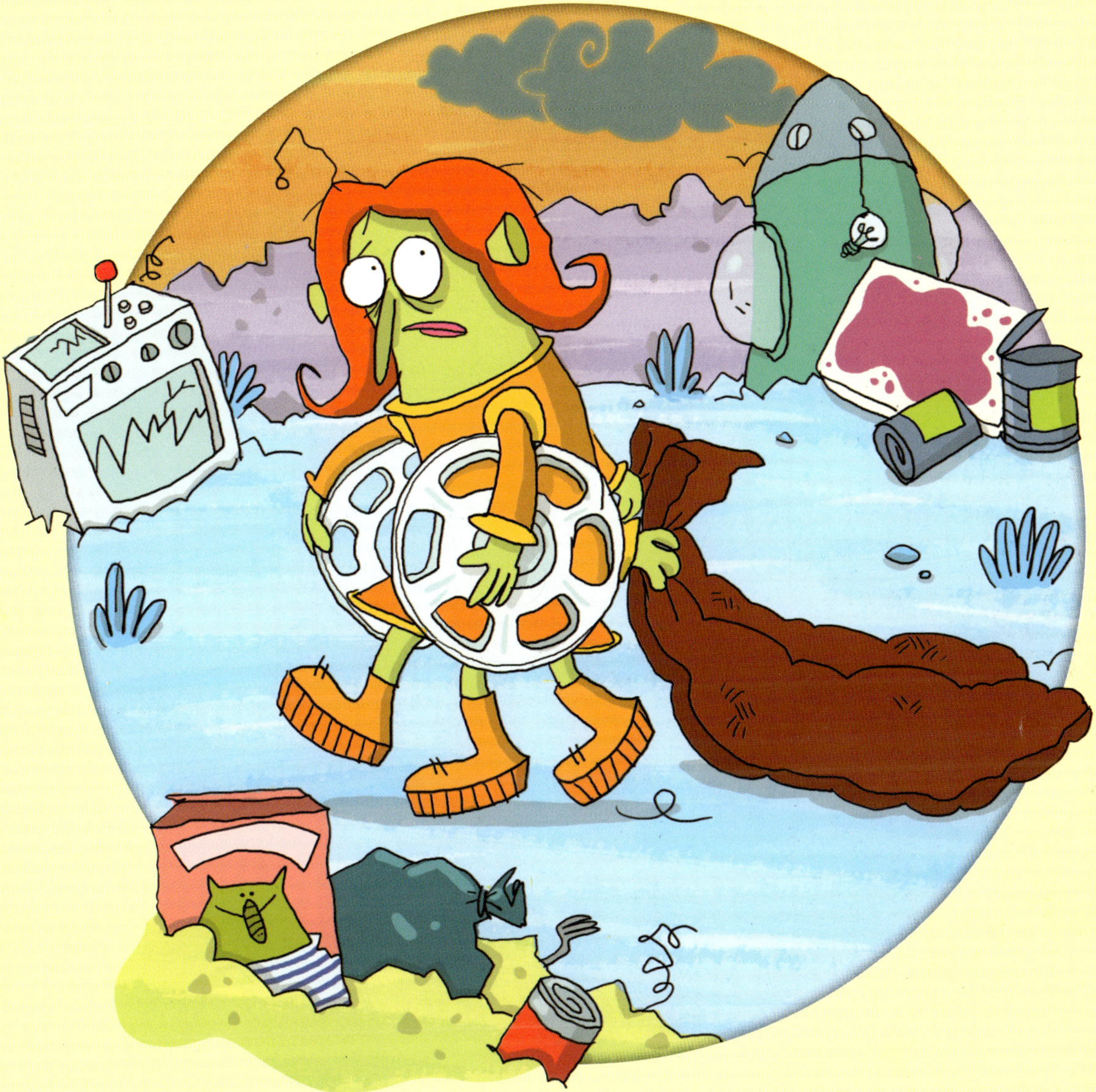

Kat got caps and mats.

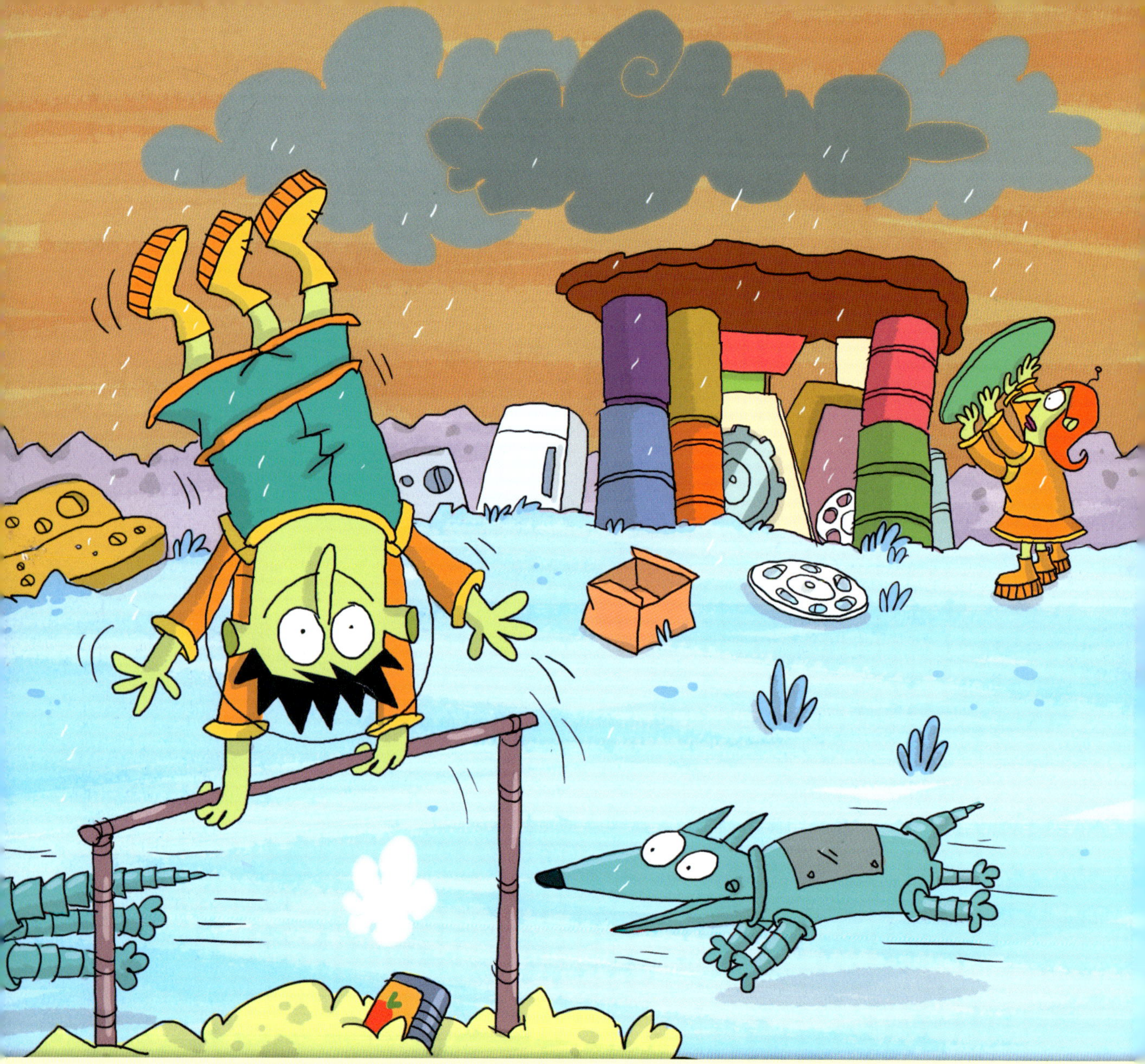

Dan did not.

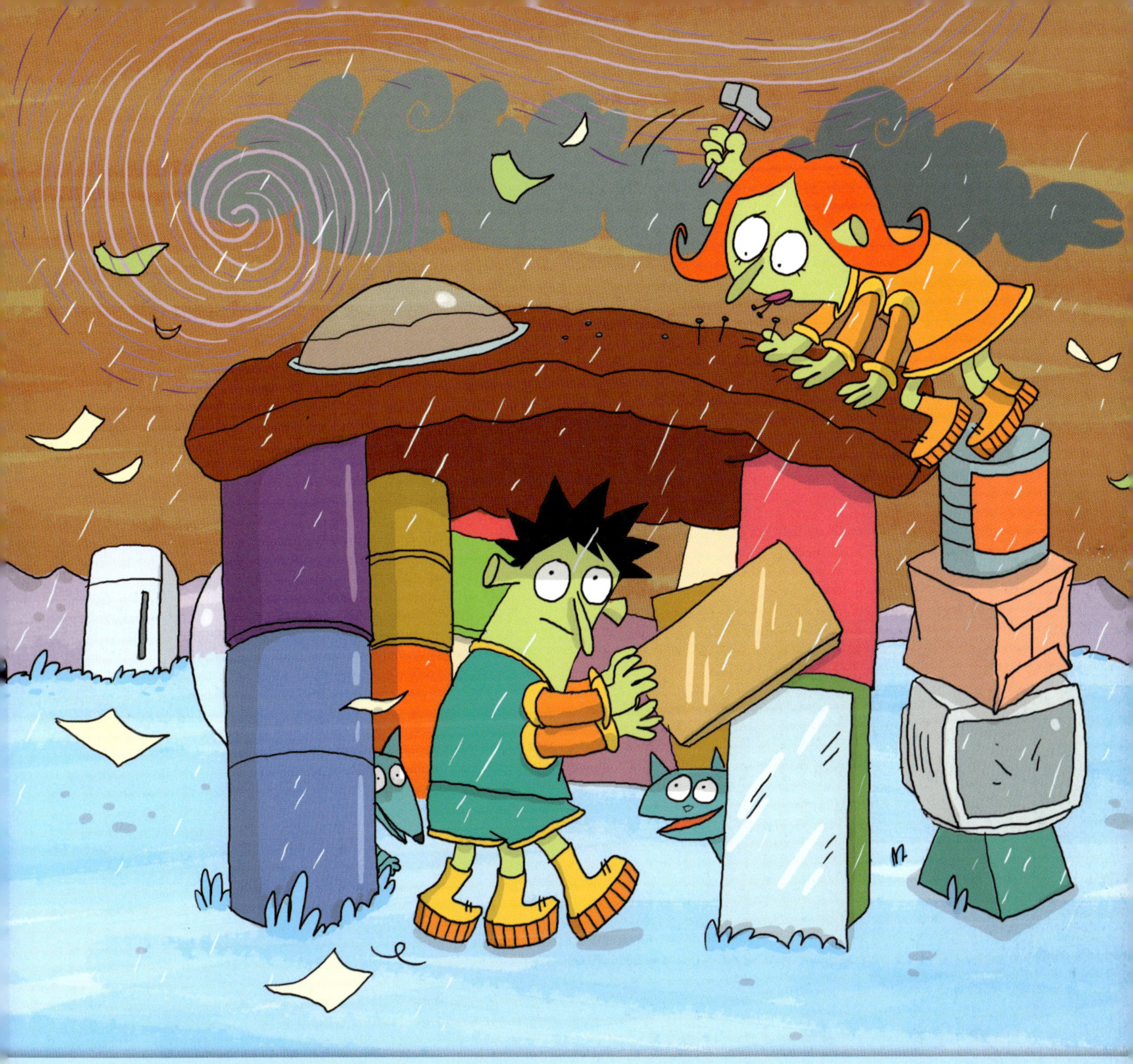

Dan got in.

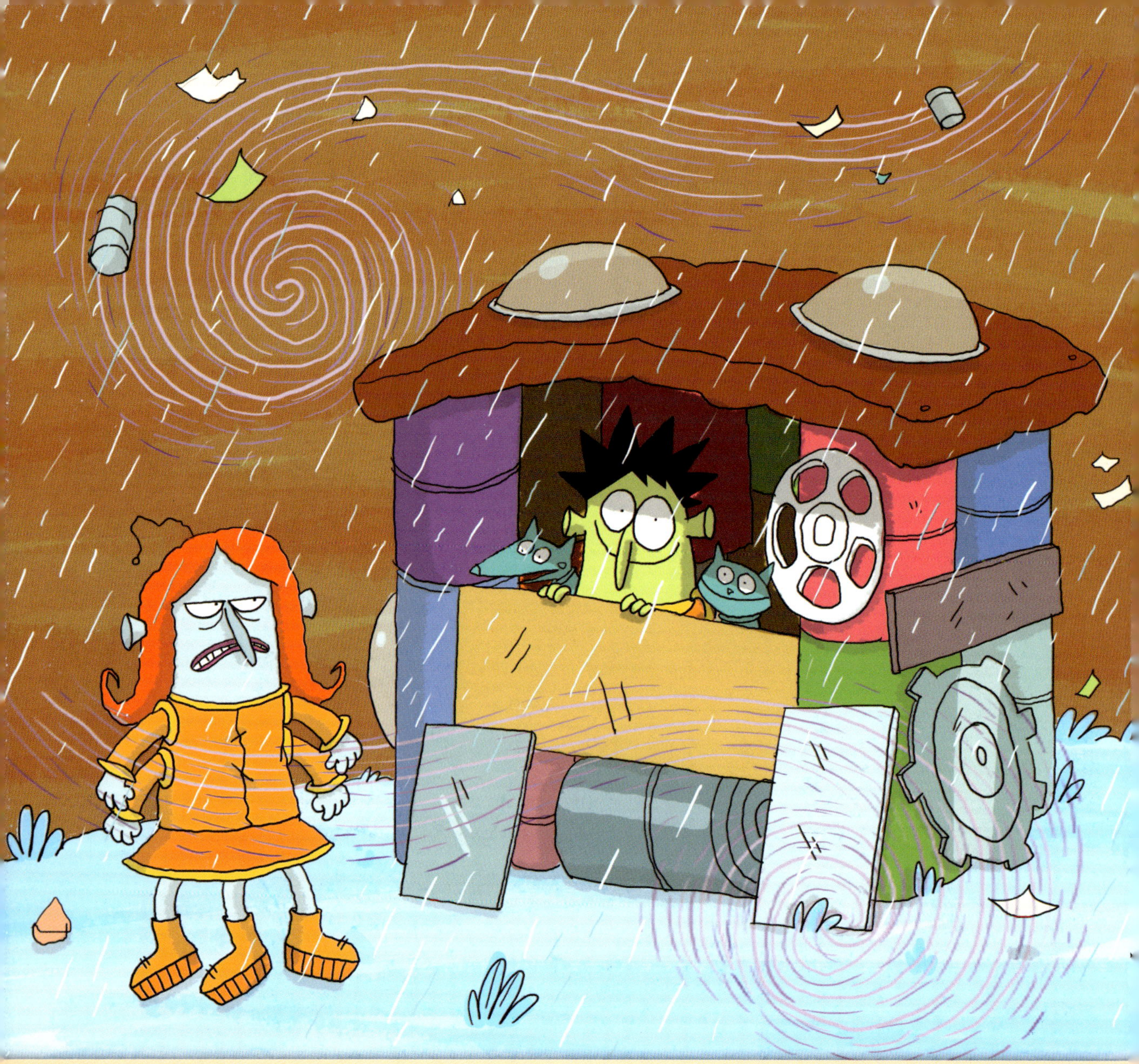

Kat did not!